Mouthfuls of Space

Also by Tom Prime

A Strange Hospital (Proper Tales Press, 2017)
Gravitynipplemilkplanet Anthroposcenesters (with Gary Barwin; above/ground press, 2019)
Birds are the birthmarks of flight and Throat Fixtures: The Almanack of Dazzle (with Gary Barwin; Serif of Nottingham, 2019)
A Cemetery for Holes (with Gary Barwin; Gordon Hill Press, 2019)
Common Stock (Blasted Tree Press, 2020)
Bird Arsonist (with Gary Barwin; New Star, forthcoming 2022)

Mouthfuls of Space

Tom Prime

an imprint of Anvil Press

Copyright © 2021 by Tom Prime
All rights reserved. No part of this book may be reproduced by any means without the prior written permission of the publisher, with the exception of brief passages in reviews. Any request for photocopying or any other reprographic copying of any part of this book must be directed in writing to ACCESS: The Canadian Copyright Licensing Agency, 69 Yonge Street, Suite 1100, Toronto, Ontario, Canada M5E 1K3

"a feed dog book" for Anvil Pres

Anvil Press Publishers Inc.
P.O. Box 3008, Station Terminal
Vancouver, BC V6B 3X5
www.anvilpress.com

Imprint editor: Stuart Ross
Cover design: Rayola.com
Interior design & typesetting: Stuart Ross
Author photo: Amelia Does

feed dog logo: Catrina Longmuir

> Library and Archives Canada Cataloguing in Publication
>
> Title: Mouthfuls of space / Tom Prime.
> Names: Prime, Tom, author.
> Description: Poems.
> Identifiers: Canadiana 20210260122 | ISBN 9781772141856 (softcover)
> Classification: LCC PS8631.R5505 M68 2021 | DDC C811/.6—dc23

Printed and bound in Canada

Represented in Canada by Publishers Group Canada
Distributed in Canada by Raincoast Books; in the U.S. by Small Press Distribution (SPD)

The publisher gratefully acknowledges the financial assistance of the Canada Council for the Arts, the Canada Book Fund, and the Province of British Columbia through the B.C. Arts Council and the Book Publishing Tax Credit.

Contents

Working Class / 9
Useless / 10
Talking to You Dead about You Being Alive / 11
Red Rose of Blushing Baby Cheeks / 11
The Advil Salesman / 12
A Strange Hospital / 13
Limb-Tree / 14
Refrigerators / 14
Glass Angels / 15
Addictionary / 21
I Held Your Hand / 22
Alien Saucer Headlight / 23
The Sun in a Box / 24
Factory / 25
The Fog and the Farmer / 25
Capitalist Mysticism / 26
General Labour / 27
Nanaimo / 28
The Green Turtle Man / 29
A Sunken Home / 30
Awaiting the Glacier's Return / 31
Siddhartha / 32
Thin Glow Schizotypal / 32
Revelations / 33
Answering Machine / 35
Morass / 35
Hold Me, Does That Sound Pathetic? / 36

Re-membered / 37

I Woke Up Behind a Baseball Diamond / 38

The Streetlight Sagged in the Stream / 39

Monkey-Paw / 40

Smoke / 41

Heaven / 42

On Our Way / 42

Pieces of My Brain / 43

Orange Fence / 44

He Hit Me in the Head with a Baseball Bat / 45

By the River in Ithaca / 46

Enlightenment / 47

Not Homeless / 48

By the Thames / 49

The Fence Factory / 50

Golden Apples / 51

A Man with a Hole in His Stomach / 53

Immurement / 54

Second Quarantine This Week / 54

Interstate 11 / 55

The Bus Light / 56

Daniel / 57

The Hubris of the Tongue / 58

Two Mouths inside My Feet / 59

A Bilabial Nasal / 60

Sleeping under the Scientology Sign / 61

Max / 62

Untitled / 62

Of the Night / 63

Town and Country / 63
Christmas Poem for Amelia / 64
Trauma Mind / 65
Saanich Bridge / 65
Mirrors / 66
Settlers / 67
Colonies / 67
The King of Eating Starlight / 68
Jezebel / 68
Everloiterer / 69
Scalpel / 70
The Bivalviad / 71
A Skeletal Lamp / 72
Riding a Bus / 73
A Hole / 74
Bees / 74
My Supervisor / 75

Working Class

I died a few years ago
since then, I've been
smoking cheaper cigarettes

I like to imagine I'm still alive
I can smoke, get drunk
do things living people do

the other ghosts think I'm strange
they busy themselves bothering people

turning on lights, opening kitchen cabinets

some try to talk to me
they think I care

about their trivial complaints
their many disappointments

Useless

He sees the scabs; they smile back at him. They are better than Seinfeld; he tells me I'm doing it all wrong. Cut up the vein, not across. Cut up the vein, so stupid, he thinks.

Talking to You Dead about You Being Alive

you told me I would move on, but it
felt like a lie, something you say

at a funeral. I'd seen you
when I was drunk—naked
throwing chairs at the wall

your head separated from your body—
swamp gases of Roswell crawled

Red Rose of Blushing Baby Cheeks

a tar-man
a million eyes
chains me
to a bike rack

I give birth:
a large sword
of butterflies

The Advil Salesman

my head is a flickering light bulb
people become irritated
their heads flicker too

Pfizer is happy about this ripple effect
they've sponsored me—"cause more subtle
pain," they say. the cheques arrive

Thursdays usually—unless I'm in
too good a mood

A Strange Hospital

last night I cut my finger off; it didn't
bleed much. I went to the hospital

it was a strange hospital; various different
appendages—thumbs, toes, arms, hands—hung on
laundry line, attached by string. the nurse mocked

me when I said I needed the finger to play
piano. I felt confused, wanted it
sewn back on—she refused, seems they were collecting

fingers and body parts to hang from laundry line. there
were many metallic instruments, blood and orange peels,
everywhere. the bed felt wormy but looked

like any other hospital bed. I was surrounded by
thick orange fence that I spend eight hours a day five

days a week cutting. a greyness hung over
everything—the face of a dead friend

Limb-Tree

cold rain shoves me to the factory
six-twenty a.m.
the production line: a human limb-tree

we are all silent in its oil womb

Refrigerators

       went to work
       across town
       the murky shut-down
       morning streets

       people's eyes
       refrigerators
       filled with meat

Glass Angels

I

irradiated by nuclear waste,
glass angels melt

I see them float sloppily
formless fingers and eyes

it's hunting season again; the buck lottery was lost
but I've been allowed to kill
one four-headed dog who represents Bargain Mart

hell has four corners; at each a man
smokes a cigarette; his skin sallow, diseased

if you look beneath
Medusa's chin, there's a glowing orange cube

it controls the nether regions of the universe

I'm suet from the carcass of a factory
feed me to hyenas dressed as real estate agents

if I cut off my penis, it'll turn into an effigy

if I plant it in soil, a clone of myself will grow
I'll have to make certain to weed

II

packs of stray dogs
hunting for half-children or the few remaining squirrels

occasionally, I see them walking down mud roads

I've been alone since my son slipped through the ice
a river of bloated timorous whale-hyenas
looking for tinfoil and wax paper

we are bombarded by neutrinos
this is what causes the common cold

I don't miss my son

I pillage sneakers from the dead
can't imagine they'd care

sometimes their spirits come to me
their heads of gold, eyes of ash
floating in blackness

the mushrooms growing on the side of the dent-road
taste like silicon

I've hammered holes into my skull
the air tickles my brain

I see colours and smell oranges
when the rain falls

remember my particle accelerator womb

III

I've found a pet—a stray dog
rare as a Cepheid binary
we walk through glass streets

a dome of emerald around us
we see holograms selling cigarettes
their stomachs filled with microchips

I don't bother smoking—my lungs
paper bags tumid with rotting vegetables
my dog's name is Rusty, after my son

automated taxis drive through the city

land-squids squirm around my tent
rubbery condom-like heads
wiggling in their own secretions

now that my son is inside me, he
commands me

"you must cut off your ear and feed it to Rusty.
Rusty will learn to hear what you hear"

the moon is a massive casino
everyone with money who didn't die
went there—my dog and I search

for glass angels, misshapen ghost-like
things—one spoonful of dark matter
will turn a half-man into a demigod

with my mind I create cities and sex objects
food to fill Rusty and me

I sometimes think of cutting out my tongue
feeding it to Rusty. he'd learn to speak

I'd like to feed Rusty my penis—
he'd feel my aching desire: I used

to fuck the transmuting latex holes
connected to massive pink blobs
vibrating like the tops of parasols

these machines were popular
now they sit stinking, strange mushrooms
covering the surface

IV

I'm growing decrepit and old—

I drink the water; it's oily. leeches
fuse to skin, become permanent
fixtures, grow into tumours
to pop and bleed out

my face, a dead husk, a snake that slithered away
my dog is good, hears thoughts

we search the stinking black sands
belching bone-mouths

we trudge across fields of hornet tails
planted by hyper-intelligent computer processors—
the moon, a Las Vegas in the sky

glow-worm light synthesized with the reflective
sub-surface of cats' eyes—a faint mist
the smell of melting plastic

dark matter in a tube of magnetized
uranium. the veins in my hands grow fibrous
and wooden—Rusty and I breathe
eyes, shadows sewn to faces

we see as one two-headed oracle
the stars burn away into blackness

an antiquated figure of civilization

a world of bodies producing brain-berries
draped from the branches of their genitals
earlobes and uncut umbilical cords

Addictionary

apathetic, I sit for hours on

my seething mattress
formed from the hide

of a nurse's soft hand.
without the pinprick

my pet entertains itself, watches me
describe hallucinations in scattered

figurative language

has a warm furry belly I rub
wordlessly. its tail

releases an aroma, blocks dopamine

receptors. life is a ship that fell
off the earth and now

floats silently in space

I Held Your Hand

walked a fog over the German Club's
half-melted January waterfront

petrified by the raw-bone cheeks of god, two
police cars idled languid as alligators

under a crippled Moses-tree. we
walked for hours past ice-mud rivers. hot

sun. apple trees exist in purgatory
halcyon chickadees chirped bright

blossoming bloodroot

Alien Saucer Headlight

my grandpa fell down in the snow
his whole body collapsed
face turned grey
eyes like the earth
from the moon

he read my Emily Dickinson
book last night
told me in the morning
he was glad she was dead
I said she probably was too

the paramedics came
I almost fainted
had my spirit sucked out of me
by some alien saucer headlight
so strange to see him hours later
at the hospital
thought his face would be a ghost's
thought I'd see him
float in the falling snow

The Sun in a Box

you can roll up
the fields of flowers
put the sun in a box

sweep the stars
underneath your bed—there's

really no use for any of it, now
that another good
man is dead

Factory

I looked across the field of weeds
the tumour-trees
I sat on the picnic table
beneath vats of
spewing plastic

couldn't imagine that
any other factory
ugly as they are
could hold more hope than this

The Fog and the Farmer

    the fog only spoke
    when it was hungry
    the farmer
    screamed at the fog

    the farmer was a ghost
    crying in the fog

    the fog ate the farmer

Capitalist Mysticism

I'm an extra in a cellphone
commercial. we all smile

clapping our hands—there are fortune-
tellers selling the past at half price

an old man with a dowsing stick
watches, as I breathe through

a vacuum. I am awarded the chance to die
smiling, clapping my hands

General Labour

just a few more words
before my time's up
there's drugs upstairs
painkillers fill my head with hazy
confused congeries—I wait
beneath the funeral grey for pickup
rain's falling subtly
this life's all I have; I hate

not having my brain to think
wet air on scratched hands—box dust

Nanaimo

before Christmas came
the puke-bellied men
waited in soup kitchens
eating the memory of their mothers

a broth of coyote and caribou
of angry crows cawing at snow foxes

The Green Turtle Man

to lie there
among the Canaanites
is to lie in a pool of old
women's hair

the white-dwarf
rain is thousands of eels
stapled to the sky

against the river-stone
I sacrificed

two headless pigeons

A Sunken Home

into a sunken home of seaweed and
rotten meat—the place where all the people I've been
live. They carry out their

lives swimming to the supermarket,
watching late-night television while floating
etc. I am forever reminded of

their many eccentricities—always searching for
pity, grandiosity, obsequious love. I am

embarrassed by the pretentious hackneyed things
they say—the drugs they dissolve themselves in.
I look at all of them gathered together

some dumb as apes, and sigh—cutting plastic fence

Awaiting the Glacier's Return

heroin, its gift of half-death, beckoned—a pale ghost's hand
the blue lips; the heart, a metronome at a slow tick

ran naked downtown screaming Crackety Anne
cars drove by in the night-rain—nobody gave a shit

the memories blur—rain on a transport
truck windshield—trying to get me to suck his dick

fucked up and hungry—dumb and pathetic
living under a bridge in Saanich
dirty socks on my hands

Siddhartha

I sit on the picnic table and eat rice,
beans, veggies, sausage—drink my iced tea and read

Hesse. The machines

scream and retch in the background—can hear the cogs
of fence-making and see the omnipresent plastic fog
possessing the concrete floors and aluminum-sided brick walls

like some vast and angry incubus

Thin Glow Schizotypal

>   your body is endlessly cloning itself
>   in the Petri dish of my heart
>
>   my voice loops inside my stomach
>   two hearts, beating out of time

Revelations

It was May, and I was sick of Toronto. Living in a squat with some friends. Since the winter had ended, I decided to hitchhike to Algonquin Park and go camping. I packed up my torn blue hitch-hiker's backpack and hit the road.

I was trying to not smoke pot for three weeks, so I had no weed, but I brought a plastic container full of Peter Jackson tobacco and a mickey of vodka. My backpack was full of stolen food (about three days' worth)—I cooked with a propane stove. By the time I got there, it was late, so I drank a bit, smoked, fell asleep on the beach.

In the morning, I stole an aluminum boat—rowed across to somebody's cottage. I read Revelations for the bizarre imagery and got bit by horseflies. I was alone. It felt good. Nobody to please, to prove myself to. It rained two nights before I left, so I sat inside my stupid child's tent and shivered in my sleeping bag while the rain leaked through.

In the morning, my matches had been destroyed, so I forced open the window of the cottage and climbed inside. A woman with a dog's head stared at me; she wore a thick see-through shawl with embroidered white elephant patches.

That night I couldn't sleep. At three or four, I packed up my sleeping bag and tent—rowed away from the island. The morning was quiet—the sky a scintillating green, due to apoplectic solar winds. All I could hear was my paddle, dipping in and out of the water, a loon calling to nothing. The mother-shadow of trees, the old light of vibrating stars.

Answering Machine

the bus is exactly as late
as I am; I sit on
the bathroom floor, still wasted
while it drives slowly on.

falling down the stairs
the night before
falling through a cloud

until waking on a bathroom floor
dumb fog of OxyContin
put my head against the haunted

air of hallucinated forms
I shiver, cold
the opposite of being born

Morass

        the pond is a mixture of cough syrup
        white wine, and canola oil
        blackened branches reach through the muck
        a pathway of Himalayan salt
        marks the direction—a velvet-winged moth
        stalks creepily behind, darkening ground

Hold Me, Does That Sound Pathetic?

Dad left me at the kid's party, I didn't even know the kid, and he went off, drink-breathed, the muglit memories a hunter's dream. His real estate agent was the guy hosting the party. He shot me full of booze, forgetmedrugs, and my first bump of cocaine—six-year-old fuckthing. I'm still out there drinking a beer, and dad's into the wine, leaving his shit all over the place—his shrimp sitting on an orangey-blood-cocktail-smudged plate. Is this the smell of history eating the slumface of its own tail? I looked at him earlier, didn't recognize myself in him. Those five years—the drugs and weirdos, waking up with snow falling at my feet, centimetre-thin free Salvation Army sleeping bag.

He didn't contact me once. Now I'm out here in the field, and he's back there treating my home like it's his. I think he left me there sometimes, because I had new shoots growing out my eyelegs that could walk up hills he didn't believe existed.

Re-membered

my arm fell off—it was my left
wasn't too bothered; lost my right leg

had to hop around—people gawked
blood gushed out—"I'm only missing two limbs"

my tongue fell out—it began to lick
people up—"what can I do? I'm not

my tongue"—on a granular hill
a sand-woman danced

I Woke Up Behind a Baseball Diamond

I hadn't heard of Sacramento until I got dropped off there by an old woman from Seattle and her son with Down's syndrome. On the I-5, at the tip of California, they were the only people who didn't look like they went to the gym every day.

Sacramento had all the lumpy streets and Western Unions one would imagine in any forgotten U.S. town. Reminded me of a brighter more brain-damaged Red Hook.

At the Western Union I called my mom. She sent some money, as the sun began to creep down, the pink of the sky salmon gutted.

Crack didn't interest me then. Crack and cracks in the sidewalk, and the cracked old pervert with his cracked skin who wanted to have a drink with me so long as I came into his metal-fingered hands and fucked him. For a little crack.

The screen door hummed with refrigerator innards. I stared too long at the dead bugs and became a skinhole to be inserted into. The grass, beneath my feet, was brittle-shaded, resembled my sun-bleached dirty blond hair. I was under his semenfeet, something he could lizardbelly, he could sweat all over—stinktongue. I was young.

The Streetlight Sagged in the Stream

The kids were nice, wore the chalk-paleness of suburbia. They broke us out each two lines, blue as the bottom of a Travelodge pool.

I don't remember what they said. The night whirred, stream was a million eyes. Late autumn, heaven's compassion-deep skies bottomless above a world gone frail.

Monkey-Paw

a man-shadow
nailed to the electric box
outside my building

mouthfuls of space
dripped from his
neck. A gasoline amoeba
strung him up
like a cheshire cat

when I turn
my hair falls off
dressed in fog
the shit-sperm windows
mumbling
loud

Smoke

I felt so good this morning
the trees waved shiny leaves

ate a perfectly ripe plum
the purple meat
lightning sweet

worked all day—little fears crept
in. I kept coughing—maybe I have cancer

the night ended, murky and smoke-filled
went to Tim Horton's
having missed my bus
bought a hot chocolate and doughnut

Heaven

I was a small town—almost happy
people used pieces of me to build homes
their children played baseball with my leg bones

last night, a tiny nuclear bomb
exploded beneath my fingernail
lit with a ruby, lathed with down

On Our Way

there are lights everywhere—like luminescent cat
eyeballs. No words are spoken—just our bodies

edging forward in time, waiting to be released. Factory
work is a form of time travel; if we did nothing but

give ourselves over to the plastic machines, we would
not need friends or family—we'd be on our way to eternity

Pieces of My Brain

I went to work with pieces
of my brain dripping out my
ears—they dripped

all over the orange
fences I cut, but I
continued to work.

I felt certain I
was bleeding out
of some hidden black hole

behind my left eyeball—nobody
talked for hours; the smell
of plastic disappeared

Orange Fence

the vents, old wizened cigarette mouths
breathe out polyethylene—I pretend

I'm interested in hanging around, like
the job interests me, like I want to spend forty
long years that blur together

cutting cheap plastic fence
don't let on that this dead-end job will float away
like the fumes of the orange fence I cut

He Hit Me in the Head with a Baseball Bat

Steve grinning like a slit throat, a car speeding down the road. Mom wouldn't have believed me if I'd told her. Eggshells had partially formed birds in them. It didn't happen. Pink-nosed green rabbit vanished.

My bed didn't know what the rubbing meant. Didn't happen. Steve tied a cable tie around Max's tail. Dragged me from the gas cap and handed me matches. What didn't happen? An orange jug, Max's rigid bony skeleton thing.

Cried into my blankie. You are lying.

By the River in Ithaca

hanging out with a recently released
heroin addict who'd only
share if I was a seventeen-
year-old girl.

the Ithacanian forest as dense
as the homeless populace.

I set up a tent just beyond the falls
felt mouse being hunted by owl
fear, so I smoked and drank

watched the glow worms, little
humming refrigerators

Enlightenment

Thought for sure there were aliens
attached to meeveryone's heads
we'd opened a portal from Saturn
my fingernails were sharp—I cut

a hole in space—crying in morning
shadow, they kept electrocuting
my toes; the walking naked acid
outside the apartment—mini-vans

drove by; a tulip talked to me
those Shams—the aliens—hung around
air-conditioner ducts. in winter
the heaters. had long tentacle hair

electrical cord and poppy milk
lightless orbs of ether—white dwarf
stomachs magnetized by car-part glands
you could cup them in your palms

Not Homeless

thirty dollars in my bank account
wouldn't have bothered me if I was
on the street, curled up under rat-bridges; now
I have a pull-out, a cat, a hibiscus
plant. used to think I
was blessed when I'd find a full cigarette
on the street. my nose ran, slimy
down my bone-face—one slop church meal

a day. probably made more money
begging than I earn selling old video
games these days. with ODSP things changed
no one molests me
no one punches me in the nose
still, I want to complain

By the Thames

if I close one eye, I can't see
the highway, but I can still hear the cars
closest I get to being
Wordsworth—daisies stupidly sway to
the east; hissing geese shit on the grassy banks
of this polluted river; still the sun-sky
is blue, the spring trees pollinating

The Fence Factory

I sat out on the picnic table
reading the final pages of *Siddhartha*
I fought to pin the pages from the wind

even the trees seemed to bend as old men's backs.
the sky was disappointed—I worked for hours

cursing at the nothing—the endlessness
of orange fence, how it didn't care to stop for me
when I failed it, how it collected in disorganized obstinate

clumps before me—fighting pointlessly, swearing

Golden Apples

when the birds flew north
and the snow became raindrops
and the hills grew gowns of green grass
we hitched on a highway

to valleys of cacti
where scorpions haunted
a fog of dust—we picked golden
apples, smoked strong pot

the tent and all our things
washed away—all our shit
pulled under the gardener-
snake stream—quivering lips

slept in a cheap hotel
the bed a foreign thing

the mid-September air
under our starving skins
my cigarette smoke and pawnshop
fur coat kept me picking

farmers' fruitage. soon it
was all rotten or sold
the birds flew south
my parents got divorced

we travelled through wet snow
waited outside McDonald's—
for spare change, plastic pancakes
the dead Thunder Bay sun

if I loved you, it was
then. your pea-green coat and
fucked-up hair—staring out nowhere
your cold October hands

A Man with a Hole in His Stomach

wants to learn about the customs
of the Swiss; he's purchased

many history books, incense sticks
a pet mongoose who serves
ham to his dripping mouth. he

sings to a formless deity. toad eyes
revolve around a bakeneko altar

Immurement

I'm a large Tupperware container filled with bones

doctors will restructure my body
cover it with polyethylene

I'll pretend to enjoy being beautiful

Second Quarantine This Week

      the factory is a tumour
      grown out of torn-up earth
      beside railway tracks

      I sit at lunchtime
      watch trains
      move slowly past

Interstate 11

I only had the road—no one's tongue. It spoke like a pack of horses panicking in the intestines of a deathbed alcoholic. Guy next to me drank so much Listerine, couldn't get a needle in. My blood kept clotting. Heard nurses shuffle in—muffled angels.

The Bus Light

he told me to take off

all my clothes. And the bus light dissipates
in the gloom—the speed of

light. He ran his sweaty
fingers down my back. The bus
screeches like a hovering

bat—no halo, no crown of dead flowers

the tick of the clock

shoving his cock. A
video camera—menacing glass

eye—collected the light

Daniel

Daniel, the poor ascetic kid
in grade three, ocean
green eyes—filled with dreams

loved Kraft Dinner and spoke in poetry.

he wore a ratty green-and-white
striped T-shirt over skinny ruddy

flesh, snot stains on the

shoulder. When he drove my
remote control car off a cliff—his eyes
opened wide as tulips blooming

The Hubris of the Tongue

the tongue talks to itself
mumbles, shakes its head

the throat is its apartment building
the throat wants back payments
has called the police

the tongue is homeless
lives in empty cigarette packs
slips through the streets

a snail without a shell

Two Mouths inside My Feet

have caused quite a stir
compelled other foot-mouths to appear

the pain of these mouths has created
business for the local podiatrists—they sew

the mouths shut, but soon the hooked
teeth and strong foot-jaws break

the meagre bonds. I rarely leave
the house now; sit in the darkness

ears filled with wax
I stuff their mouths with cotton balls

gobs of pre-chewed bubble gum;
soon their baying echoes off the walls

A Bilabial Nasal

my computer coding skills are limited
so I've designed a system of baked goods
I colour with various edible inks

I move these muffin-like shapes around
a flattened cardboard box with a picture
of a microprocessor on it

Sleeping under the Scientology Sign

too late for morning to dress me in
rags of Vancouver's mildewed

crack-teeth twilight. the lachrymose
rain falls
against slabs of sidewalk

bagged people, impotent as geldings
stagger down Hastings

Max

holding my breath
until I turn blue

my dead dog
he speaks through
a mouth in his pupil

Untitled

        the dead leaves
        crackling on the ground—
        arthritic elderly bodies

Of the Night

the grass is green mud hair
everybody wet-faced
I could go to my friend's
walk through the closed-down hooker streets—March rain falling

could drink a glass of red wine
monosyllabically
the rain coughs in the wind
a petulant thief sleeping at truncated corners of concrete

what could I find down there?
thrown-away lottery tickets
dogs on chains with hard grrs—the rest of the skeleton parade

Town and Country

      a man sings karaoke funeral
      off pitch—murky stars
      in his half-moon eyes. in the oily
      cloud-filled streets, a gnarled

      double-man tree hunches by the neon window
      his eyes, rivers without sky

Christmas Poem for Amelia

an invasive plant species has attached
itself to my hypothalamus
I am constantly producing dopamine

the Queen is a thousand-year-old
lizard. it's Christmas and I ate a lot

I bought you a baby grizzly bear
put it in a refrigerator
box. but by morning, it had scratched free

Trauma Mind

I'm a robot coated in dog fur
skin, velvet carpet

I'll see a girl murdered
after I'm ass-raped
she'll sew up my stomach
a vagina pinned together

the highway is the throat of an angel
a receding staircase

Saanich Bridge

        I wake up feeling rain in my throat
        transport trucks
        rattle the oily underbelly bridge
        stream of bloated diapers
        grocery carts and smoke packs

        I shit by it—pants stained with ketchup
        some kids walk past and laugh; hide my dick
        pull up my pants
        roll butts and smoke blackened tobacco
        rain mixed with wet snow

Mirrors

I felt this strangeness, brumous
rivers, ribbons on my old guitar—when

leaf shadow tree light punched me in the nose—
where flowers, like one-sided mirrors, grow—

blood would flow gently over wintry frozen
earth.

Settlers

we have gods here
there are bones
we pump through pistons

welcome

we have nice vistas—we'll
offer you shiny buttons

take your females, your
precious metals

your fetishist alien porn
appeals to us

Colonies

how boring
late-night television

the frog spat out
the mouth
of a madwoman
walled in with boxes

The King of Eating Starlight

I am his six-year-old
neon dog-legged whore

he sews wolf-ears
onto my head
removes layers of lake-mist

Jezebel

I drilled a hole in my skull
thinking that helium
would be released
there was no helium

a small clown with Styrofoam teeth
climbed out, laughing
he pulled behind him
three dogs
one had the face of god

Everloiterer

a man with a shrunken, dried
gorilla intestine fishing pole
lived in a pothole on the gorilla-
hide road. he fished
in the dead leaf-puddles for mitochondria

he resided on the terraformed body
of Enkidu: the cosmic gorilla

with Big Macs assembled by robots
and computerized fields of vegetables
farmed by subservient dog-men
there was no work on earth.
clearcutting the forest

gorilla fur provided space to colonize

Scalpel

my friend carried me in his palm
he said, "aren't I strong!"
I said, "I'm only ten pounds"

the path rusted
children, skipping rope, grew old
glaciers crept into their bones

I stood in a doorway
watching women float
one had a scalpel

she moved in reverse
I stabbed out her temple
whole cities of skin

she had eaten my eyes
her stomach was glass
the moon fell into the ocean

The Bivalviad

a clam in the sky opens
miniature turkeys walk out

one large headless turkey
composed of infinite
microscopic turkeys

in turn made of infinite
smaller decapitated turkeys

born in unison from the sky-clam

A Skeletal Lamp

hidden underneath its
icy surface: long-necked

Modigliani monsters hugging
beneath the hardened sky

their love, a skeletal lamp. They

don't know Jupiter or space—stars
asteroids and all that—just the
complete black

like those skull fish swimming
in the lower intestine of the ocean

scaly Klimt diamond gods
free of the knowledge
of anything—Europa

Riding a Bus

if death were anything more than dirt and nothingness,
it would be like riding a bus—the phosphorescent lights are
flickering and need to be replaced—down an endless reaching

highway—the yellow lines pierce like migraine hallucinations. It

would carry every version of each person—the air is muggy and
hard to breathe—from childhood onward. No one would
ever speak—there are never any hitch-hikers

outside and no one plays cards or reads

A Hole

there is a
hole in
the side of my
head. I pick at it and
it grows—

it has
grown so large

there are trees
flowers

so large, a
moon orbits

Bees

        fingers pressed
        into meat cubes—

        I have fed them
        bees from a kicked nest

My Supervisor

my supervisor is a drunk
rides a forklift, has tall bleached hair
such a skinny malnourished
face: looks
like it has begun to implode. I had

a vision of him
running along the rolling lines
of orange fence and finally, after growing old
inertia and decay
crept up in the form of

a mastic-slicked black snake
and trapped his legs. He
was pulled into the vortex
of hardened chemicals
swallowed by the winding and
inexorable plastic fence manufacturing machine

Dedicated to Jackson my cat.
Even though if he were alive, he wouldn't care or understand this,
he was my best friend and my only real family for the worst part of my life.
I will always remember him

Acknowledgements

Poems from this collection have been published in *Carousel*, *Fjords Review*, *The Rusty Toque*, the Proper Tales Press chapbook *A Strange Hospital*, and elsewhere.

This book would not have gotten written without excellent suggestions by Kathryn Mockler, Madeline Bassnett, Shane Book, and Tim Lilburn. My partner, Amelia Does, helped me push through the process of editing this book and not giving up on it. Gary Barwin provided useful insight that helped develop the earliest draft of this collection. Obviously, Stuart Ross has been instrumental in getting this book published. Thanks all for believing in me and putting up with all those awful poems that got cut!

Tom Prime is in the PhD program at Western University in English. He has an MFA in Creative Writing at the University of Victoria (Specializing in Poetry) and a BA at Western University. He is also a songwriter and performer. Access his music at holdenmain.bandcamp.com. Tom lives in London, Ontario.

Other Feed Dog Books from Anvil Press

"A Feed Dog Book" is an imprint of Anvil Press edited by Stuart Ross and dedicated to contemporary poetry under the influence of surrealism. We are particularly interested in seeing such manuscripts from members of diverse and marginalized communities. Write Stuart at razovsky@gmail.com.

The Least You Can Do Is Be Magnificent: New & Selected Writings of Steve Venright, compiled and with an afterword by Alessandro Porco (2017)
I Heard Something, by Jaime Forsythe (2018)
On the Count of None, by Allison Chisholm (2018)
The Inflatable Life, by Mark Laba (2019)
Float and Scurry, by Heather Birrell (2019)
The Headless Man, by Peter Dubé (2020)
Queen and Carcass, by Anna van Valkenburg (2020)
il virus, by Lillian Necakov (2021)

an imprint of Anvil Press